PIANO SOLO

MARVEL STUDIOS

AVENGERS
ENDGAME

MUSIC FROM THE ORIGINAL MOTION PICTURE SOUNDTRACK

T0081878

ISBN 978-1-5400-5993-2

Images and artwork © 2019 MARVEL

MARVEL COMICS MUSIC, INC.

Visit Hal Leonard Online at
www.halleonard.com

Contact us:
Hal Leonard
7777 West Bluemound Road
Milwaukee, WI 53213
Email: info@halleonard.com

In Europe, contact:
Hal Leonard Europe Limited
42 Wigmore Street
Marylebone, London, W1U 2RN
Email: info@halleonardeurope.com

In Australia, contact:
Hal Leonard Australia Pty. Ltd.
4 Lentara Court
Cheltenham, Victoria, 3192 Australia
Email: info@halleonard.com.au

CONTENTS

SCOTT LANG

TOTALLY FINE

Music by ALAN SILVESTRI

Moderately slow

PERFECTLY NOT CONFUSING

Music by ALAN SILVESTRI

THE HOW WORKS

Music by ALAN SILVESTRI

Cool Swing

ONE SHOT

Music by ALAN SILVESTRI

THE TOOL OF A THIEF

Music by ALAN SILVESTRI

PORTALS

Music by ALAN SILVESTRI

Moderately slow

THE REAL HERO

Music by ALAN SILVESTRI

MAIN ON END

Music by ALAN SILVESTRI